Table of Contents

PRESIDENT BARACK OBAMA PARTICIPATES IN A TWITTER #MY2K LIVE QUESTION AND ANSWER SESSION IN THE ROOSEVELT ROOM OF THE WHITE HOUSE, DEC. 3, 2012. (OFFICIAL WHITE HOUSE PHOTO BY PETE SOUZA)

"This isn't about faster Internet or fewer dropped calls. It's about connecting every part of America to the digital age. It's about a rural community in Iowa or Alabama where farmers and small business owners will be able to sell their products all over the world. It's about a firefighter who can download the design of a burning building onto a handheld device; a student who can take classes with a digital textbook; or a patient who can have face-to-face video chats with her doctor."

- President Obama, State of the Union Address, 2012

Introduction

Broadband access is an essential part of our economy. Given the reliance of so many American businesses and families on this basic technology, it's easy to overlook that just 15 years ago broadband barely existed for consumers.

To create jobs and grow wages at home, and to compete in the global information economy, the delivery of fast, affordable and reliable broadband service to all corners of the United States must be a national imperative. The build-out of broadband infrastructure itself is a major driver of American investment and job creation, but even more significant are the ways that connectivity is transforming a range of industries, from education to entertainment to agriculture to travel. High-speed wired and wireless networks place the United States at the center of a digital economy that is one of the brightest parts of our short-term recovery and long-term competitiveness.

This report highlights (1) the status of broadband development in the United States in 2013, including both progress made in achieving greater availability to broadband as well as the significant remaining challenges of timely and affordable deployment of broadband to all Americans; (2) several important contributions of the Obama Administration over the last four years that have accelerated the growth of broadband technology; and (3) two key opportunities for further action.

I.   The State of American Broadband in 2013

By nearly any metric the last four years have been a period of tremendous growth in broadband infrastructure, access, and the digital economy upon which they rely.

Since the President took office, national broadband availability has increased at all advertised speed levels.[1] Today, about 91 percent of Americans have access to wired broadband speeds of at least 10 Mbps downstream, and 81 percent of Americans have access to similarly fast mobile wireless broadband.

The last four years have also been a period of significant transition in the needs of many broadband subscribers. Taking advantage of low barriers to entry and an open network, providers of cloud computing, remote processing, media-rich content and streaming video have created unprecedented demand for higher-bandwidth Internet services to businesses and households alike. That demand has driven substantial investment in high-speed facilities.

The government commonly defines the "basic" speed for broadband at 3 Mbps downstream and 768 kbps upstream (3Mb/768kb), with some regulatory decisions defining basic service as 4 Mbps downstream and 1 Mbps upstream.[2] Nonetheless, we acknowledge that the country is rapidly reaching the point at which baseline broadband evaluations should increase, and might instead begin at 10 Mbps downstream.[3] This evolving baseline reflects a growing need for increased bandwidth as more Americans use the Internet for work and to build career skills.[4]

Changing attitudes about broadband also track with the growth in demand and availability. The number of broadband adopters continues to increase steadily, alongside the rising number of Americans who consider the Internet a valuable learning tool. In 2011, 77 percent of American Internet users ages 25 and older reported relying on the Internet for personal communications,

---

[1] National Telecommunications and Information Administration. "U.S. Broadband Availability: June 2010 – June 2012." May 2013. Available at http://www.ntia.doc.gov/report/2013/us-broadband-availability-june-2010-june-2012. (Hereafter, NTIA, May 2013).

[2] E.g., the Federal Communications Commission has defined broadband for certain regulatory purposes to mean downstream speeds of at least 4 Mbps and upstream speeds of at least 1 Mbps. Sixth Broadband Report, 25 FCC Rcd 9556, 9563 ¶10 (2010).

[3] Since these lower baselines were used in developing most broadband metrics to date, when determining the "cutoff" for broadband, data throughout this report reflects those earlier metrics. While we believe 10 Mbps downstream is an increasingly "basic" speed, setting a 10 Mbps baseline for future evaluations does not imply that such speeds will fully meet all or even most Americans' needs. As upward evolution in broadband speeds continues, however, reaching that figure at affordable prices should be a low-end standard.

[4] See, for example, U.S. Small Business Administration, Office of Advocacy. "The Impact of Broadband Speed and Price on Small Business." Columbia Telecommunications Corporation, November 2010. Available at: http://archive.sba.gov/advo/research/rs373tot.pdf.

while 66 percent relied on it for general information – and about half depended on the Internet for financial services, for consumer services and for entertainment.[5]

While broadband access and speed have grown significantly over the last four years, significant areas for improvement remain, as the FCC has documented.[6] Moreover, many markets are subject to at most limited competition among broadband providers.[7] Thus, areas for improvement remain. Ongoing efforts are needed to ensure that all Americans have access to affordable and reliable high-speed access – and that the infrastructure exists to support increases in consumer and business demand for higher speeds.

Figure 1: The Transformation in American Connectivity[8]

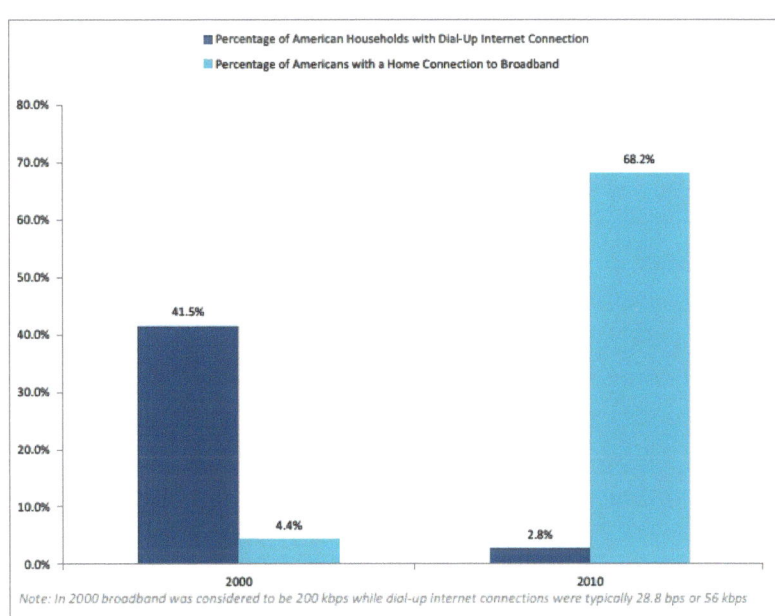

Significant Private Investment

Responding to the increasing consumer demand for services accessed through broadband, the private sector has been driving important advances in infrastructure and technology. U.S. telecommunications firms have made significant investments in infrastructure; for example,

---

[5] National Telecommunications and Information Administration & Economics and Statistics Administration, "Exploring the Digital Nation: America's Emerging Online Experience." June 2013. Available at http://www.ntia.doc.gov/report/2013/exploring-digital-nation-americas-emerging-online-experience. (Hereafter, NTIA & ESA, June 2013).

[6] Federal Communications Commission, "Eighth Broadband Progress Report.," (August 2012). Available at: http://hraunfoss.fcc.gov/edocs_public/attachmatch/FCC-12-90A1.pdf.

[7] Open Internet Order, 25 FCC Rcd 17905 ¶32 (2010).

[8] National Telecommunications and Information Administration, "Digital Nation, Expanding Internet Access, NTIA Research Preview," February 2011. Available at http://www.ntia.doc.gov/files/ntia/publications /ntia_Internet_use_report_february_2011.pdf.

just two of the largest U.S. telecommunications companies account for greater combined stateside investment than the top five oil/gas companies, and nearly four times more than the big three auto companies combined.[9] In fact, since President Obama took office in early 2009, nearly $250 billion in private capital has been invested in U.S. wired and wireless broadband networks. In just the last two years, more high-speed fiber cables have been laid in the United States than in any similar period since 2000.[10] Moreover, during President Obama's first term, the annual investment in U.S. wireless networks alone grew more than 40 percent from $21 billion to $30 billion. Projections for 2013 estimate an annual wireless network investment at $35 billion.[11]

These investments in broadband, along with the openness of the network, are part of a self-perpetuating cycle that coupled with increased broadband adoption and digital literacy skills training, have significantly improved access to higher-speed wireline and wireless broadband services, brought new users online and enabled the "App Economy," a phenomenon that itself has driven demand for and deployment of even faster high-speed services.

High-Speed Wired and Wireless Access for More Americans

Evaluating the United States' progress in broadband access requires a careful weighing of a number of characteristics, including access, speed, and geography. Measured against these factors, digital networks in the United States have improved greatly from even just a few years ago, reaching a larger percentage of households and offering much faster speeds.

Fast Speeds. The figure below displays the most recent broadband-speed availability data from the National Telecommunications and Information Administration (NTIA).

Figure 2: Percentage of U.S. Population with Access to Various Advertised Broadband Download Speeds (Mbps)[12]

	≥ 3 Mbps	≥ 6	≥ 10	≥25	≥ 50	≥ 100	≥ 1 Gbps
All Broadband	98.18%	96.17%	94.39%	78.51%	75.15%	47.09%	3.17%
Wireline	93.41%	92.81%	90.91%	78.11%	74.85%	46.87%	3.17%
Wireless	94.37%	84.17%	80.66%	4.94%	3.03%	1.80%	0.00%

---

[9] Progressive Policy Institute, "Investment Heroes." July 2012. Available at: http://progressivepolicy.org/wp-content/uploads/2012/07/ 07.2012-Mandel_Carew_Investment-Heroes_Whos-Betting-on-Americas-Future.pdf.
[10] FCC, "Significant actions and key developments in the Broadband Economy," 2013. Available at: http://webcache. googleusercontent.com/search?q=cache:Arky8AO3ehwJ:transition.fcc.gov/Daily_Releases/Daily_Business/2013/d b0322/DOC-319728A1.doc+&cd=2&hl=en&ct=clnk&gl=us. Deployment of fiber optic cable includes of combination of middle-mile and last mile coverage, thus the increase in new infrastructure may not align with the increase in the availability of broadband via fiber to the premises.
[11] *Ibid.*
[12] NTIA May 2013.

Notably, wireless (mobile and fixed) broadband has demonstrated remarkable gains in availability, and wired broadband access continues to improve. Even with 93% availability, however, millions of Americans remain without access to fixed broadband, which often provides the most robust connections. As described below, the Commerce Department and the Federal Communications Commission have made progress, and are taking numerous important steps to address this challenge through a number of ongoing programs.

Figure 3: Percentage of Population with Access to Broadband Speeds by Technology Type[13]

	≥ 3 Mbps / 768 kbps	≥ 6	≥ 10	≥25	≥ 50	≥ 100	≥ 1 Gbps
Cable	86.92%	86.95%	86.15%	76.42%	72.63%	44.20%	0.00%
DSL	73.51%	64.60%	47.39%	7.21%	0.11%	0.01%	0.00%
Fiber	20.20%	20.00%	19.86%	18.72%	18.25%	6.79%	3.16%
Fixed	34.33%	25.81%	10.89%	4.88%	2.99%	1.78%	0.00%
Mobile	91.81%	80.58%	78.67%	0.00%	0.00%	0.00%	0.00%
Copper	43.25%	15.37%	14.59%	1.46%	0.27%	0.12%	0.01%

Leading Wireless Technology. With the deployment of fourth-generation (4G) technologies such as Long-Term Evolution (LTE), advanced mobile broadband service is also much more widely available today than it was two years ago.[14] The most recently available data from NTIA (June 2012) indicates that 80.6 percent of Americans now have access to advanced mobile broadband.

To place those figures in context, not only was the United States the first country to deploy 4G LTE networks at scale, but also, as of mid-2012 nearly half the world's LTE subscribers were within the United States.[15] Likewise, in 2012, North America's average mobile data connection speed was 2.6 Mbps – the fastest such average in the world, nearly twice that available in Western Europe, and over five times the global average.[16]

---

[13] NTIA, May 2013.

[14] LTE and HSPA+ are two types of Terrestrial Mobile Wireless technologies that offer faster speeds than previous generations and are typically considered "4G" in marketing materials. For more information about technology types, see http://www.broadbandmap.gov/classroom/technology.

[15] IDATE Research. "LTE 2013: Markets & Trends, Facts & Figures."

[16] Cisco, Global Mobile Data Traffic Forecast Update, 2012-2017. We note that this report does not compare countries on a country-by-country basis. Akamai's State of the Internet report (below) includes mobile speed data by provider, but not by country. Page 31 of that report shows that of the three mobile providers studied, the average mobile data connection speeds were 1.4 Mbps, 2.6 Mbps and 4.6 Mbps. The fastest mobile provider with the fastest speeds in the world is located in Austria and provides average data connection speeds of 8 Mbps.

The average connection speed in the United States in the fourth quarter of 2012 was 7.4 Mbps, the eighth fastest among all nations, and the fastest when compared to other countries with either a similar population or land mass.[17]

Platform for Innovation, Growth and Consumer Benefits: Smartphones, Tablets and other Internet-Connected Devices

As of the first quarter of 2013, 500 million Internet-connected devices were in American homes.[18] These include smartphones, tablets, and other Internet-connected devices that run applications. Between 2009 and 2012, U.S. smartphone ownership increased from 16 percent to 56 percent.[19] More than 80 percent of smartphones sold globally in 2012 run operating systems developed by U.S. companies, up from 5 percent six years ago and 25 percent three years ago. Moreover, a growing number of households have transitioned away from wired phone lines, and the number with only mobile phones today exceeds 35 percent.[20]

These devices have done more than connect Americans to one another more easily. The integration of mobile broadband, advanced operating systems and increasingly sophisticated hardware, along with low barriers to entry to an open network, have enabled an entire economy of mobile applications to develop in the United States. This "App Economy" is one of America's most dynamic and growing sectors, and one that industry studies have cited as creating more than 500,000 U.S. jobs since 2007.[21]

Economic studies have also placed the "consumer surplus" or value consumers gain from their time online at roughly 2 percent of their income – a particularly impressive outcome given that Americans spend a tiny fraction of that amount to get broadband service.[22] It is easy to imagine why: another study found that in answering everyday questions, those who had access to a search engine did so in fifteen fewer minutes than those without Internet access.[23]

The benefits are not just for the individual and household. Broadband is known to make a substantial contribution to national economic growth, as more and more citizens become

---

[17] Akamai, The State of the Internet, 4th Quarter, 2012 Report, http://www.akamai.com/stateoftheInternet/.

[18] NPD Group, "Internet Connected Devices Surpass Half a Billion in U.S. Homes, According to the NPD Group." March 2013. Available at: https://www.npd.com/wps/portal/npd/us/news/press-releases/Internet-connected-devices-surpass-half-a-billion-in-u-s-homes-according-to-the-npd-group/.

[19] Aaron Baar, Market Daily. "Tablets, Smartphones Driving CE Sales," July 2012. Available at: http://www.mediapost.com/ publications/article/179415/tablets-smartphones-driving-ce-sales. html# axzz2UeuoHIJv. Also FCC, "Significant actions and key developments in the Broadband Economy."

[20] CDC Wireless Substitution. Available at:http://www.cdc.gov/nchs/data/nhis/earlyrelease/wireless201212.pdf.

[21] TechNet, February 2012. Available at: http://www.technet.org/new-technet-sponsored-study-nearly-500000-app-economy-jobs-in-united-states-february-7-2012/.

[22] Austan Goolsbee and Peter Klenow, "Valuing Consumer Products by The Time Spent Using Them: An Application to the Internet," National Bureau of Economic Research, January, 2006.

[23] Yan Chen, Grace YoungJoo Jeon, Yong-Mi Kim, "A Day without a Search Engine: An Experimental Study of Online and Offline Searches," University of Michigan, March 6, 2013.

empowered to take advantage of innovative technologies and connect to each other in new ways. Subsequent study of that consumer surplus suggests that Internet access contributed to the economy an average of $34 billion per year since 2002 (equivalent to about 0.26 percent to annual GDP growth).[24] A separate study of 25 OECD countries between 1996 and 2007 found that a 10 percent increase in broadband penetration raises per-capita GDP growth by 0.9-1.5 percentage points. Another study found that within 66 high income countries during the period 1980-2002 a 10 percent increase in broadband penetration yielded an additional 1.21 percentage points of GDP growth.[25] Increasing the speed of a nation's broadband connectivity also provides an economic boost – a study of 33 OECD countries between 2008 and 2010 concluded that doubling the broadband speed for an economy increases GDP by 0.3 percent.[26]

Significant Challenges Remain: Adoption, Speed, and Pricing

Today, more than 56 percent of Americans have a smartphone,[27] and more than 78 percent of Americans are Internet users. However, 72 percent of Americans use broadband at home. Despite the advances in broadband coverage – particularly considering the United States' size and geography – adoption is lower than in some nations with comparable Gross Domestic Product (GDP) per capita.[28] Connecting more homes in the United States remains an important policy priority; absent this connectivity, individuals cannot take advantage of opportunities for education and skills development, entrepreneurship and e-commerce available to those with the connectivity.

Given the promise that broadband connections hold for households, businesses, and the economy as a whole, low adoption, availability of higher-speed connections, and affordability remain concerns for national broadband policy.

Uneven adoption. Demographic factors influence broadband adoption. For example, home broadband adoption among those with at least a college degree (88%) is more than double that of those who did not complete high school (35%); 50 percentage points separate broadband use of households with annual incomes exceeding $100,000 from those with incomes below $25,000 (93% compared to 43%). A larger percentage of urban dwellers use broadband at home (72%) than rural residents (58%), while Asians (81%) and Whites (74%) have adopted broadband at home to a greater extent than Hispanics (56%) and African Americans (55%).[29]

---

[24] Erik Brynjolfsson and Joo Hee Oh, "The Attention Economy: Measuring the Value of Free Goods on the Internet."

[25] "The Impact of Broadband on the Economy." International Telecommunication Union, April 2012.

[26] Ericsson, Arthur D. Little, and Chalmers University of Technology, 2011.

[27] Aaron Baar, Market Daily, July 2012. Available at: http://www.mediapost.com/publications/article/179415/tablets-smartphones-driving-ce-sales.html#axzz2UeuoHIJv.

[28] OECD Broadband Portal, Table 1d(2). June 2011. http://www.oecd.org/dataoecd/21/35/39574709.xls.

[29] NTIA & ESA June 2013.

In total, approximately 29 percent of Americans do not use broadband at home as of 2011 – this includes 8 percent of Americans who access the Internet only away from home (for instance at the workplace or an anchor institution such as a library or community center) and less than 3 percent of Americans who continue to use dial-up at home. Why do millions of these Americans who have access still choose not to subscribe? According to recent surveys, cost, skills and relevance remain major concerns.

Figure 4: Percentage of Broadband Adoption by Demographic Group[30]

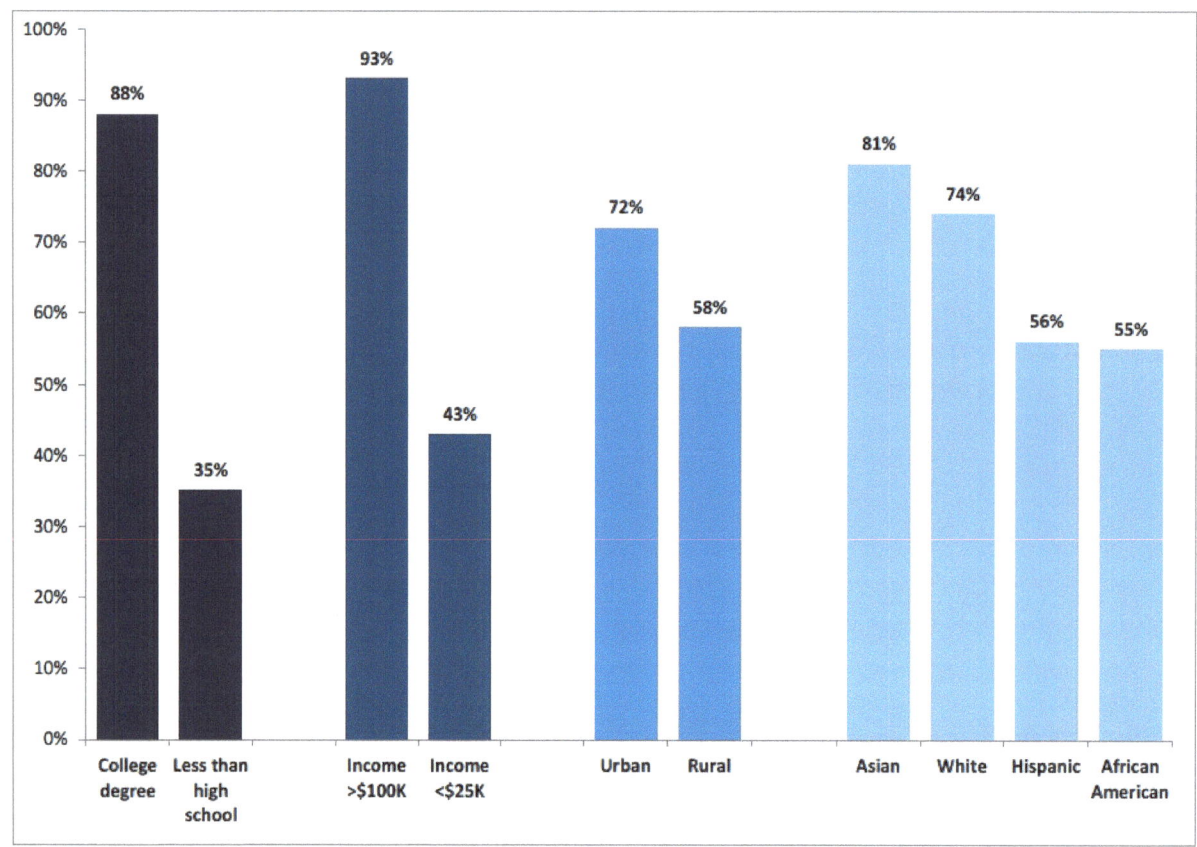

Lack of Interest. In 2011, almost half of all households that did not use the Internet at home reported they had no need or interest in going online. This was especially true for older Americans; 68 percent of Americans 65 years or older were likely to express no need or interest in using the Internet at home, compared to 21 percent of people between the ages of 16 and 44.

Those who frequently visit the Internet report using it for a variety of purposes. In 2011, users at least 25 years of age stated they rely on the Internet for: personal communications (77%); general information (66%); entertainment (48%); job searches, job training, or working from

---

[30] NTIA & ESA June 2013.

home (29%); healthcare (27%); and education or schoolwork (23%), among others.[31] NTIA's Broadband Technology Opportunities Program (BTOP) public computer center projects are helping to teach non-users about these benefits to encourage them to adopt this empowering technology. These surveys are corroborated by international data suggesting that broadband use in schools drives home adoption; in Portugal, for instance, students in schools with high-speed broadband were 20 percent more likely to adopt broadband at home.[32]

Affordability. The second most common reason cited for lack of broadband adoption is affordability. In 2011, 28 percent of non-adopting households did not have broadband service at home primarily because of the expense of Internet service, an increase of four percentage points above 2010 data. Cost represents a significantly greater obstacle for lower income Americans: compared to 18 percent of households with annual incomes above $50,000 that cited affordability as the main deterrent to going online, 32 percent of families with incomes below $25,000 responded that the high cost of Internet service prevented them from using broadband at home.

The cost of broadband varies significantly based on speed, type of service package, and geographical location; the data about those costs also varies significantly. Based on a limited sample of prices available on provider websites, the FCC reports that in 2011 dollars, the average monthly price for a 1-5 Mbps connection was $35, the average cost of a 5-15 Mbps connection was $44, and the average price of a 15-25 Mbps connection was $56.50.[33] The cost of "triple-play" packages (Internet, TV, and phone) also vary. New America Foundation found that plan prices in the United States started at $66/month for a basic package that included broadband speeds of 6 Mbps downstream and 1 Mbps upstream as well as TV and phone service. At the higher end, symmetrical service at 30 Mbps coupled with phone and TV was $130/month. For a stand-alone wireline service, price varies significantly depending on location and provider. At around $35, for example, a customer in San Francisco can subscribe to a 200 Mbps symmetrical connection; New York and Washington, D.C., residents can subscribe to a 25 Mbps down/2 Mbps up service; and citizens of Los Angeles can purchase a 10 Mbps down/1 Mbps up service.[34] Most data indicate the price consumers pay has remained steady or increased year-to-year, even though speed is increasing for those base prices over time; thus price remains one of the key challenges to increasing broadband adoption in the United States.

In addition to increasing adoption rates, the United States must also prepare for the increasing need for faster speeds by consumers, businesses and community anchor institutions. While broadband is accessible through multiple technologies at lower speeds, far fewer technologies

---

[31] NTIA & ESA June 2013.

[32] Rodrigo Belo, "Broadband in Schools: Effects on Student Performance and Spillovers for Household Internet Adoption." 2012. *Dissertations.* Paper 105. Available at: http://repository.cmu.edu/dissertations/105.

[33] FCC, "International Broadband Data Report." Available at: http://www.fcc.gov/document/international-broadband-data-report.

[34] New America Foundation, "The Cost of Connectivity." July 2012. Available at: http://oti.newamerica.net/publications/policy/_the_cost_of_connectivity.

offer the faster speeds necessary to take full advantage of emerging innovations (see below).[35] For example, while cable, DSL, and mobile wireless are all widely available at basic broadband speeds, at 25 Mbps, only cable (76.42%) is widely available, followed next by fiber (18.72%).

Figure 5: Percentage of Population with Access to Top-Tier Broadband Speeds[36]

	≥25 Mbps	≥ 50	≥ 100	≥ 1 Gbps
Cable	76.42%	72.63%	44.20%	0.00%
DSL	7.21%	0.11%	0.01%	0.00%
Fiber	18.72%	18.25%	6.79%	3.16%
Fixed Wireless	4.88%	2.99%	1.78%	0.00%
Mobile	0.00%	0.00%	0.00%	0.00%
Copper	1.46%	0.27%	0.12%	0.01%

While it is a positive development that users often have the opportunity to choose among wired and wireless services at basic speeds, high-speed connections continue to show room for improvement both in availability, cost, and competition, particularly as more homes, companies and community institutions require higher speeds.

Disparity Between Urban and Rural Access

Figure 6: Broadband Availability by Urban and Rural (June 2012)[37]

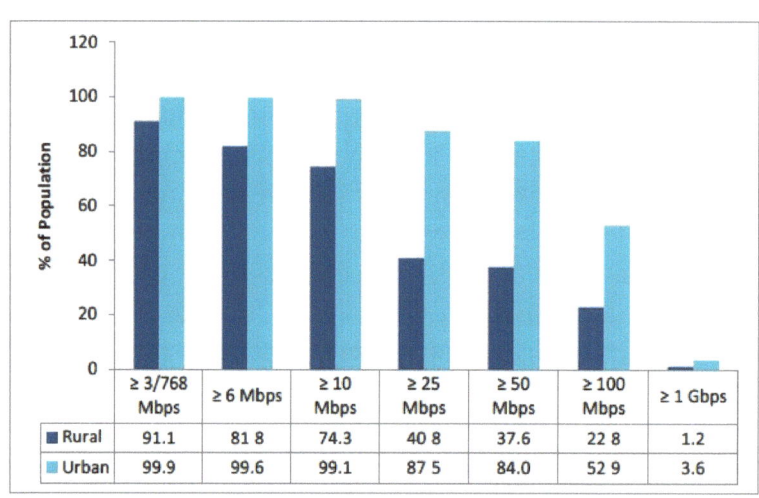

	≥ 3/768 Mbps	≥ 6 Mbps	≥ 10 Mbps	≥ 25 Mbps	≥ 50 Mbps	≥ 100 Mbps	≥ 1 Gbps
Rural	91.1	81 8	74.3	40 8	37.6	22 8	1.2
Urban	99.9	99.6	99.1	87 5	84.0	52 9	3.6

---

[35] This graphic, available at http://ctcnet.us/DataSpeeds.jpg, provides a visual depiction of the speed capabilities of various types of broadband technology.

[36] NTIA May 2013.

[37] The U.S. Census Bureau categorizes each census block in the country as either "rural" or "urban." The criteria defining the 2010 Census urban areas are available at http://www.census.gov/geo/www/ua/fedregv76n164.pdf; see also http://www.census.gov/geo/www/ua/uafaq.html).

Of great concern is also the disparity between urban and rural access, as well as uneven distribution of high-speed access across certain underserved geographies. Today, while almost 100 percent of urban residents have access to download speeds of at least 6 Mbps, only about 82 percent of residents in rural communities can access those speeds. The disparity is even more pronounced at higher speeds: almost 88 percent of urban residents have access to speeds of 25 Mbps, but less than half that percentage, about 41 percent, have access to those speeds in rural communities. Of course not all users require those higher speeds, and satellite and terrestrial wireless technologies continue to deliver promising improvements. But even considering the higher costs often associated with providing broadband to rural areas, limits in availability should not hold back rural populations seeking higher-speed, high quality Internet access.

Access to broadband in rural communities also differs considerably by state. In 10 states and four territories, 20 percent or less of the rural population has access to speeds of 25 Mbps. In 15 states and Puerto Rico, between 21 percent and 40 percent of the rural population has access to speeds of 25 Mbps. In only 12 states do more than 60 percent of their rural populations have access to at least this speed.[38]

Figure 7: Percent of Population in Rural Areas with Access to 25 Mbps Speeds[39]

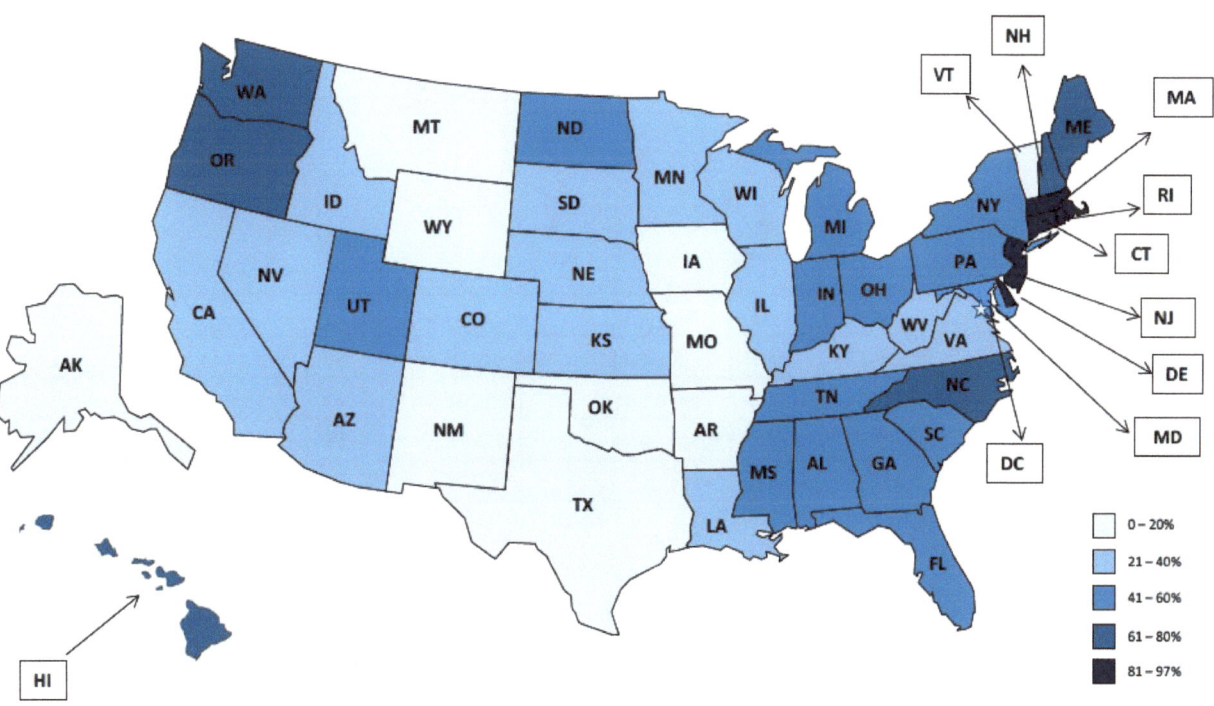

---

[38] The District of Columbia is not included in these figures because all of its population is urban.
[39] NTIA May 2013.

The tables below highlight those states with the greatest broadband access at the middle three tiers of available speeds, as well as those with the least such access.

Figure 8: 15 States with Most Broadband Access at 10, 25 and 50 Mbps[40]

	Most Access: ≥ 10 Mbps			Most Access: ≥ 25 Mbps			Most Access: ≥ 50 Mbps	
1	DC	100%	1	Rhode Island	99.62%	1	Rhode Island	99.62%
2	Rhode Island	99.80%	2	Connecticut	99.09%	2	DC	98.27%
3	Connecticut	99.75%	3	DC	98.44%	3	Connecticut	97.08%
4	New Jersey	99.48%	4	New Jersey	97.77%	4	Hawaii	96.94%
5	Delaware	99.29%	5	Hawaii	96.94%	5	Massachusetts	96.55%
6	Massachusetts	99.16%	6	Massachusetts	96.84%	6	New Jersey	96.37%
7	Maryland	98.99%	7	Delaware	95.81%	7	Delaware	95.78%
8	Hawaii	98.70%	8	Washington	95.28%	8	Washington	94.76%
9	Florida	98.47%	9	Oregon	92.73%	9	Oregon	92.20%
10	New York	98.39%	10	California	91.22%	10	New York	90.97%
11	Utah	98.35%	11	New York	91.04%	11	California	89.56%
12	Washington	98.15%	12	Florida	90.71%	12	Utah	89.22%
13	California	97.95%	13	Utah	90.71%	13	Maryland	88.91%
14	Pennsylvania	97.15%	14	Maryland	89.46%	14	Nevada	84.33%
15	Illinois	96.90%	15	Illinois	87.53%	15	Michigan	83.05%

Figure 9: Five States with Least Broadband Access at 10, 25 and 50 Mbps

	Least Access: ≥ 10 Mbps			Least Access: ≥ 25 Mbps			Least Access: ≥ 50 Mbps	
47	Wyoming	81.58%	47	Arkansas	28.54%	47	Iowa	19.81%
48	Alaska	81.40%	48	Wyoming	22.17%	48	New Mexico	10.85%
49	Mississippi	78.57%	49	Vermont	20.48%	49	Wyoming	2.27%
50	Montana	75.52%	50	Montana	12.71%	50	Montana	1.42%
51	West Virginia	69.69%	51	Alaska	0.06%	51	Alaska	0.00%

---

[40] NTIA May 2013.

II.   The Obama Administration's Contributions

> ### KEY POINTS
>
> ➤ More than $2.8 billion invested in over 220 projects that have already built and improved over 90,000 miles of broadband infrastructure and made high-speed connections available to about 14,000 community institutions.
>
> ➤ Created tax incentives to spur one of the largest private-sector infrastructure investments in history.
>
> ➤ On track to ensure that at least 98% of Americans have access to 4G wireless broadband service by 2016, and to free up 500 MHz of wireless spectrum for commercial use.

Once we emerge from the immediate crisis, the long-term economic gains to communities that have been left behind in the digital age will be immeasurable. Studies have shown that when communities adopt broadband access, it can lead to hundreds of thousands of new jobs. Broadband can remove geographic barriers between patients and their doctors. It can connect our kids to the digital skills and 21st century education required for the jobs of the future. And it can prepare America to run on clean energy by helping us upgrade to a smarter, stronger, more secure electrical grid.

-    President Barack Obama, July 2, 2010

The Obama Administration has made a number of contributions to the rapid growth of high-speed broadband, including (1) stoking broadband investment through the Recovery Act; (2) providing tax incentives for business investment; (3) freeing up spectrum for mobile broadband; and (4) a light-touch, multi-stakeholder approach to regulation that has fostered both innovation in applications and deployment of infrastructure.

Recovery Act Investment in Broadband

One important goal of the Recovery Act was to increase access to and drive adoption of broadband across America, including an important $6.9 billion upgrade to the nation's broadband infrastructure. As part of the appropriation, $4.4 billion was administered by the Department of Commerce's NTIA to deploy broadband infrastructure, support public computer centers and encourage adoption of broadband. The remaining $2.5 billion was directed to the Department of Agriculture's Rural Utilities Service (RUS) to expand broadband access in rural areas.

Under the RUS's Broadband Initiatives Program, over $1.4 billion has been awarded to 105 broadband projects in 37 states and one territory. NTIA's Broadband Technology Opportunities Program (BTOP) received more than 2,800 applications requesting more than $36 billion in support for potential projects in all 50 states and territories. Grant recipients were required to show that "but for" these Federal grant funds, there would not be a business case to serve these communities. As of the end of May 2013, NTIA had invested over $2.8 billion in over 220 projects in every state, territory and the District of Columbia, the vast majority of which has been spent building and improving over 90,000 miles of broadband infrastructure and making high-speed connections available to about 14,000 community institutions across the country.[41]

BTOP grants fell into three categories:

1. *Comprehensive Community Infrastructure.* Projects to deploy new or improved broadband facilities (e.g., laying new fiber-optic cables or upgrading wireless towers) and to connect "community anchor institutions" including schools, libraries, hospitals, and public safety facilities. These networks help ensure sustainable community growth and provide the foundation for enhanced household and business broadband Internet services.

2. *Public Computer Centers.* Projects to establish new public computer facilities or upgrade existing ones that provide broadband access to the general public or to specific vulnerable populations, such as low-income individuals, the unemployed, seniors, children, minorities, and people with disabilities.

3. *Sustainable Broadband Adoption.* Projects that focus on increasing broadband Internet usage and adoption, including among vulnerable populations where broadband technology traditionally has been underutilized. Many projects include digital literacy training and outreach campaigns to increase the relevance of broadband in people's everyday lives.

Additionally, through the State Broadband Initiative (SBI), NTIA awarded approximately $293 million to 56 recipients, one grant each to the 50 states, five territories, and the District of Columbia. With this funding, states have been collecting and validating data biannually on the availability, speed, type, and location of broadband services, as well as the broadband services used by community anchor institutions, such as schools, libraries, and hospitals. The result of this effort is a pioneering data source, the National Broadband Map (www.broadbandmap.gov) that has enabled the Administration to provide the best quality information on broadband services ever available in the United States. In addition, states are also using this grant funding to organize around broadband capacity building, using the data to drive policy and support local and regional efforts to compete in the digital economy.

These Recovery Act investments are helping to improve access to education and healthcare services as well as boost economic development for communities stymied by limited or no access to high-speed broadband. The investments in broadband infrastructure, public computer centers, and sustainable adoption have helped provide job training to the unemployed or under-employed, helped school children access the materials they need to learn, allowed rural

---

[41] For a visualization of the BTOP investments, see NTIA's Connecting America's Communities interactive map at http://www2.ntia.doc.gov/BTOPmap/.

doctors to connect to more specialized medical centers, and enabled small businesses to offer their services to national and international markets. BTOP projects, for example, have already delivered about 10 million hours of technology training to about 2.8 million users. Important lessons about how to overcome barriers to adoption are captured in NTIA's Broadband Adoption Toolkit – a further return on the nation's investment.[42]

BTOP accompanied another important development in expanding broadband access: the Federal Communications Commission's *Connect America Fund.* After a decade of unsuccessful reform attempts, the FCC voted unanimously in October 2011 to overhaul the Universal Service Fund (USF).[43] The USF was originally designed as a program for delivering telephone service to rural America; its reform created the Connect America Fund to ensure broadband access to all Americans. The Connect America Fund is a public-private partnership that will over 10 years work to extend broadband to un-served consumers and communities across the country. As part of its overhaul, the Commission also established access to mobile broadband as a universal service goal for the first time, and created the Mobility Fund to spur deployment of advanced wireless infrastructure and eliminate dead zones. In their first phases of implementation, the Connect America Fund and Mobility Fund are already helping extend home broadband to nearly 400,000 previously un-served Americans and bring mobile broadband to up to 83,000 previously-uncovered road miles.

Tax Incentives for Private Investment

Businesses making capital investments in broadband, like in other areas, are allowed to recover the cost of those expenditures over time through a depreciation expense deduction. By allowing an immediate deduction (or "expensing") of investment costs, the tax relief that the President has signed into law lowers the effective tax rate on income derived from business investments. (Expensing provisions reduce the after-tax cost of investment by allowing companies to deduct the cost of their investment in the year it purchases qualified tangible property and places that property into service, rather than stretching that deduction out based on the depreciation schedule for that investment.) This incentive increases the effective rate of return on investment, leading companies to make investments that might otherwise be unattractive.

The President signed into law one of the largest temporary tax incentives for investment in American history, which has played a key role in accelerating and increasing investment across the economy – and particularly in telecommunications. In addition to this incentive expensing that was in effect in 2011, the President also signed into law additional investment incentives every year since 2009.

---

[42] NTIA's Broadband Adoption Toolkit, May 2013. Available at: http://www.ntia.doc.gov/press-release/2013/ntia-broadband-adoption-toolkit-shares-best-practices-across-us.

[43] Edward Wyatt, "F.C.C. Overhauls a Telephone Subsidy," New York Times, October 27, 2011, http://www.nytimes.com/2011/10/28/business/fcc-overhauls-fund-for-broadband-service.html?_r=0. http://hraunfoss.fcc.gov/edocs_public/attachmatch/FCC-11-161A1.pdf

Furthermore, by providing an immediate window of opportunity in which the costs of investing in qualified property are lower, a temporary expensing policy encourages firms to accelerate investment that they might delay for several years – an especially powerful incentive for investments in longer-lived assets, like broadband infrastructure.

As part of the 2009 Recovery Act, the President allowed businesses to recover the costs of certain capital expenditures made in 2008 and 2009 – including capital investments in broadband infrastructure – faster than under the ordinary schedule, by depreciating 50 percent of the cost in the year the investor placed the property in service. The President's 2010 Small Business Jobs Act extended this first-year 50 percent bonus depreciation for qualifying property purchased and placed in service in 2010.[44]

In December 2010, the President signed into law legislation that provided immediate 100 percent expensing of investment costs, one of the largest temporary investment incentives in American history, which allowed businesses and investors to deduct immediately the full cost of broadband investments rather than having to depreciate them over time – a benefit that Treasury estimated could encourage $50 billion in total additional investment.[45] The American Taxpayer Relief Act provided 50 percent bonus depreciation for investments made in 2013.[46]

This tax incentive had an especially significant effect on the broadband industry. In a joint 2011 letter, leaders from Comcast and Time Warner described the effect expensing had on their ability to invest in broadband infrastructure: "Despite the downturn in the economy, the cable communications sector has been able to continue steady investment and to retain jobs as a result of policies like 100 percent expensing."[47] And in 2010, the Independent Telephone & Telecommunications Alliance (ITTA) released a statement commending Congress for passing the President's Small Business Jobs Act "and specifically for the inclusion of bonus depreciation language included in the Act … [which] will allow ITTA member companies to accelerate broadband investment and deliver the economic, educational, and healthcare opportunities that broadband provides."[48]

---

[44] The While House Blog, "President Obama Signs Small Business Jobs Act - Learn What's In It," Sep. 2010. Available at: http://www.whitehouse.gov/blog/2010/09/27/president-obama-signs-small-business-jobs-act-learn-whats-it
[45] The U.S. Department of Treasury, "The Case of Temporary 100 Percent Expensing; Encouraging Business to Expand Now By Lowering the Cost of Investment," Oct. 2010. Available at http://www.whitehouse.gov/sites/default/files/expensing_report.pdf.
[46] The White House Office of the Press Secretary, "Fact Sheet: The Tax Agreement: A Victory for Middle-Class Families and the Economy," Jan. 2013. Available at: http://www.whitehouse.gov/the-press-office/2013/01/01/fact-sheet-tax-agreement-victory-middle-class-families-and-economy.
[47] Kyle McSlarrow and Gail MacKinnon, letter to the Honorable John Boehner, Dec. 2011. Available at http://waysandmeans.house.gov/uploadedfiles/comcast_time_warner.pdf.
[48] Press statement, "ITTA Commends Congress for Passage of Bonus Depreciation," Sep. 2010. Available at http://www.itta.us/advocacy/2010/BONUS%20DEPRECIATION%20SBJCA%2092310%20207%20(f).pdf.

Freeing Spectrum for New Innovation

As the President stated in June 2010, "America's future competitiveness and global technology leadership depend, in part, upon the availability of additional spectrum. The world is going wireless and we must not fall behind." The need for spectrum is a constant refrain, and the Administration continues to devote significant attention to the issue.

The public policy imperative was highlighted by the Council of Economic Advisors that, in its February 2012 report, concluded, "it is unlikely that wireless carriers will be able to accommodate this surging demand without additional spectrum...In short, the projected growth in data traffic can be achieved only by making more spectrum available for wireless use."[49] Private-sector studies have reached similar conclusions, noting that wireless data traffic in North America is likely to increase 100-fold between 2009 and 2016.[50]

To address this need, in 2010 the President directed NTIA to work with the FCC to re-purpose 500 MHz of spectrum from existing Federal or nonfederal use to wireless broadband within 10 years, almost doubling the amount of spectrum available for that use. The challenge to NTIA and the agencies was a daunting one: within the spectrum bands best suited for wireless broadband service, dozens of Federal agencies operate thousands of spectrum-dependent systems supporting national defense, law enforcement, and severe weather forecasting, among other vital Federal missions. Yet within just a few months, NTIA had identified 115 MHz of federally-assigned spectrum that could be re-purposed for broadband and described its plan and methodology for reviewing additional spectrum bands to reach the 500 MHz goal. In executing upon that plan, NTIA supported the formation of working groups made up of representatives of Federal agencies, commercial broadband providers, and other stakeholders who are engaged in unprecedented collaborative efforts to free up more spectrum for the FCC to allocate to wireless broadband service while safeguarding critical Federal activities.

In parallel with these efforts, the President announced in his 2011 State of the Union address a commitment to ensure that at least 98 percent of Americans had access to 4G wireless broadband service by 2016. Thanks to private and public investments resulting from spectrum policy, tax incentives, Recovery Act investments, and competition policy, we are on track to achieve the goals of bringing 4G to nearly all Americans by the President's deadline.

Central to the President's wireless agenda are the spectrum provisions he proposed in the American Jobs Act, which were carried forward in the Middle Class Tax Relief and Job Creation Act of 2012. This legislation expanded the FCC's authority to auction spectrum, enabling more robust wireless broadband service for consumers while also raising billions of dollars in

---

[49] Council of Economic Advisors, "The Economic Benefits of New Spectrum for Wireless Broadband," Feb. 2012. Available at: http://www.whitehouse.gov/sites/default/files/cea_spectrum_report_2-21-2012.pdf.
[50] Cisco's Visual Networking Index: Forecast and Methodology, May 2013. Available at: http://www.cisco.com/en/US/solutions/collateral/ns341/ns525/ns537/ns705/ns827/white_paper_c11-481360_ns827_Networking_Solutions_White_Paper.html.

revenue. The most innovative feature of the bill is the grant of authority to the FCC to design and conduct "incentive auctions," in which television broadcasters can voluntarily bid on the right to relinquish some or all of their spectrum rights in return for some of the proceeds raised when that spectrum is auctioned for flexible use, such as wireless broadband. The FCC has proposed rules for the incentive auctions and is reviewing public comments now.

In addition to providing incentives for federal agencies sharing or relocating from spectrum reallocated to commercial users, last year's legislation also established the First Responders Network Authority, or FirstNet, an independent authority within NTIA tasked with the design and deployment of a nationwide interoperable wireless network for first responders. FirstNet will empower regional, state, local, tribal, and territorial public safety agencies with the advantages of nationwide scale and interoperability across boundaries, while also giving them local control and flexibility. At the same time, with dedicated spectrum of its own and $7 billion in funding from spectrum auctions, FirstNet will partner with commercial providers and other stakeholders to expand wireless broadband access across the nation.

In comparison to other nations, the United States ranks among the top countries in current licensed spectrum available for mobile broadband, and while we cannot predict the amount of spectrum freed by the incentive auctions, this forthcoming spectrum — combined with Federal repurposing — are likely to keep the United States well atop other nations in mobile broadband allocation.

Figure 10: Summary of Total Available Licensed Spectrum Available for Mobile Broadband (in megahertz)

Country	Current	Pipeline	Current + Pipeline
USA	608	55+	663+
Australia	478	230	708
Brazil	554	0	554
China	227	360	587
France	555	50	605
Germany	615	0	615
Italy	540	20	560
Japan	500	10	510
Spain	540	60	600
U.K.	353	265	618

Note: US pipeline numbers do not include the significant amount of spectrum that will be made available for mobile broadband from incentive auctions and federal repurposing.

Also vital to our economy is unlicensed spectrum, which is responsible for many of the innovative wireless technologies in devices we use every day, such as Wi-Fi. Last year's legislation confirmed the FCC's discretion to designate spectrum for unlicensed use, such as Wi-Fi. Unlicensed spectrum plays an important role in fostering new wireless uses by enabling "innovation without permission." Unlicensed spectrum applications have transformed the personal electronics industry, and are poised to make substantial contributions to the retail, manufacturing, and other sectors. Additionally, low power, close-range connections like Wi-Fi are essential to easing the strain on the cellular networks of the major wireless broadband carriers. Studies indicate that the majority of traffic over smartphones and tablets is now carried over Wi-Fi.[51] In comparison to the European Union, the United States has substantially more spectrum (as well as more diverse spectrum) available for unlicensed applications.

Figure 11: Amount of Spectrum Below 6 GHz Available for Unlicensed Broadband Use

Band	USA Current	USA Pipeline	EU Current	EU Pipeline (Unknown)
TV White Spaces [Unl1]	0-150	+	-	
863-870 MHz	-	-	7[Unl2]	
902-928 MHz	26[Unl3]	-	-	
1880-1930 MHz	10[Unl4]	-	20[Unl5]	
2400-2483.5 MHz[Unl6]	83.5	-	83.5	
3550-3700 MHz	50[Unl7]	100[Unl8]	-	
5150-5350 & 5470-5825 MHz[Unl9]	555	-	555	
5350-5470 & 5850-5925 MHz	-	195[Unl10]	-	
TOTAL	724.5-874 5	295+	665 5	

Light-Touch, Multi-Stakeholder Policies to Build Opportunity and Trust

The Administration has also taken a comprehensive approach to broadband and Internet policy, with a series of policies, multi-stakeholder efforts, and processes that are improving the efficiency and predictability of the digital economy. They include:

---

[51] Yochai Benkler, "Open Wireless vs. Licensed Spectrum: Evidence from Market Adoption." Available at: http://www.benkler.org/Open_Wireless_V_Licensed_Spectrum_Market_Adoption_current.pdf, p. 6.

- **FCC's 2010 Open Internet Order.** In 2010 the FCC established light-touch rules designed to ensure that the Internet remains an open platform for innovation and expression, and that content is delivered regardless of its origin or recipient. The rules ensure low barriers to entry by providers of Internet-based services, which in turn continues to stimulate demand for service and facilities by making the Internet more valuable to users.

- **Consumer Privacy Bill of Rights.** Because trust in digital systems and the companies handling personal information is essential to the economy, the Administration released the nation's first-ever comprehensive policy document on digital privacy. As part of that policy's commitment to encouraging innovation, minimizing regulatory burden, and engaging all stakeholders, NTIA has for the last year led an inclusive, voluntary process for developing privacy codes of conduct.

- **National Strategy for Trusted Identities in Cyberspace.** To help promote an ecosystem with better security than the standard username and password, the White House released the National Strategy for Trusted Identities in Cyberspace (NSTIC), and has staffed a national program office at the National Institutes of Standards and Technology (NIST) to coordinate the Federal activities needed to implement the trusted identity ecosystem. That office has been leading efforts to promote private-sector involvement, build consensus on legal and policy frameworks, work with industry to identify new standards, and promote pilot projects.

- **Cybersecurity.** In addition to the nation's first top-to-bottom review of national cybersecurity policy (the Cyberspace Policy Review), President Obama has also taken important steps to reduce the economic drag and uncertainty caused by cybersecurity vulnerabilities. Specifically, he outlined a series of legislative actions in his May 2011 Legislative Proposal, and in 2013 signed Executive Order 13636, which expanded information sharing, developed robust privacy protections, and set up an inclusive, multi-stakeholder effort to develop nation-wide standards for critical infrastructure cybersecurity.

- **International Strategy for Cyberspace.** The U.S. International Strategy for Cyberspace is the United States' comprehensive foreign policy document for the digital world, outlining our vision for sustaining a global online environment that is open to innovation, interoperable the world over, and secure and reliable enough to support our economic growth. The strategy explains how the multi-stakeholder model, free data flows, respect for Internet Freedom, and strong regulatory forbearance helps enhance prosperity globally.

- **Internet Policy Board.** To regularize the development of national policy related to the digital economy, the White House also established in early 2013 the Internet Policy Board, a senior-level forum for policy development and decision-making. The Board includes regular membership from the President's Cabinet agencies, as well as several components of the Executive Office of the President.

III. Policy Opportunities

KEY POINTS

➢ **Schools and community anchors** remain underserved, particularly at connection speeds that would support important advances in education crucial to national competitiveness.

➢ **Spectrum sharing** will be crucial to the future of wireless broadband, and the federal government should encourage the policies and technology advances to enhance it.

There are a variety of opportunities to drive the broadband agenda forward, including important priorities like promoting competition, continuing to fuel investment and innovation, and protecting consumers. This report focuses on two important areas where policy innovation can help unlock the full potential of broadband technology for Americans: expanding high-speed access for schools and anchor institutions, and continuing efforts to relieve the spectrum crunch.

Schools and Anchor Institutions

"[I]n an age when the world's information is a just click away, it demands that we bring our schools and libraries into the 21st century. We can't be stuck in the 19th century when we're living in a 21st century economy. That's why, today, we're going to take a new step to make sure that virtually every child in America's classrooms has access to the fastest Internet and the most cutting-edge learning tools. And that step will better prepare our children for the jobs and challenges of the future and it will provide them a surer path into the middle class. And, as a consequence, it will mean a stronger, more secure economy for all of us."

- President Obama, Mooresville, North Carolina, June 6, 2013

Driven by new digital technologies, the future of learning is increasingly interactive, individualized, and full of real-world experiences and information. While broadband access has improved considerably in recent years, broadband infrastructure in America's K-12 schools and local libraries has lagged far behind. Unfortunately, despite the successes of the FCC's E-Rate program connecting schools to the Internet for the first time, oversubscription means that the average school has about the same connectivity than the average American home, but serves 200 times as many users, and fewer than 20 percent of educators say their school's internet connection meets their teaching needs. And our teachers do not get enough training and support to integrate technology in their classroom and lessons, despite the fundamental and increasing importance of those skills.

According to the State Educational Technology Directors Association, within a few years schools with at least 1,000 students will need at least 1 Gbps to leverage the transformative power of online learning.[52] By comparison, in South Korea, 100 percent of schools already benefit from ultrafast Internet connections.

The limited bandwidth in America's classrooms is insufficient to support promising applications, such as online tutoring systems or graphic-rich educational games proven to increase student engagement and retention. In fact, most schools cannot support even multiple classrooms simultaneously streaming free educational resources, such as Khan Academy mini-lectures or LearnZillion math lessons. In many cases, bandwidth will also be insufficient to support the interactive tests currently planned across the country that align to the new college and career-ready standards that the Administration has promoted through Race to the Top and the No Child Left Behind reforms.

New education opportunities such as Massive Open Online Courses (MOOCs) and synchronous online learning are enabled by fast broadband speeds at universities and at home, and these education resources are changing how millions of Americans engage in postsecondary learning. With additional broadband capacity, America's K-12 students will also be able to benefit from high-speed opportunities.

Through the Recovery Act's BTOP and BIP grants, the Federal Government sought to help bolster this underserved market. BTOP grant projects will connect nearly 10 percent of all K-12 schools nationwide to networks capable of speeds in excess of 100 Mbps, the speed the U.S. Department of Education cites as a baseline to support 21st century digital learning.

In states like North Carolina and West Virginia, BTOP has been a catalyst for getting virtually all schools connected to high-speed broadband – and the impact of getting schools onto a statewide network is tremendous. In North Carolina, over 70 percent of all schools in the state which did not already have high-capacity broadband available are being connected to a statewide network via the Recovery Act – and consolidating buying power has lowered Internet access prices by about 60 percent. In West Virginia's McDowell County, schools are taking advantage of the improved access to broadband in ways that connect rural students to the entire world and provide rich, interactive learning experiences. In addition to connecting schools to high-speed networks, BTOP projects have offered courses to help teachers integrate online content into their curriculum and provided funding to support devices for students and teachers.

CFY (previously Computers for Youth) is using BTOP funding to provide digital literacy training and computers for low-income sixth graders and their families in New York City and Los Angeles. The CFY program focuses on high-poverty schools, offering Saturday workshops to teach students and parents how to use the Internet and find online educational resources that

---

[52] State Educational Technology Directors Association, "The Broadband Imperative: Recommendations to Address K-12 Education Infrastructure Needs," 2012. Available at: http://www.setda.org/c/document_library/get_file?folderId=353&name=DLFE-1515.pdf.

promote learning in subjects such as math and reading. CFY also trains families on its own PowerMyLearning.com platform, which provides free access to activities and games from across the Web that are designed to make learning fun.

The nation has an opportunity over the next few years to build on the success of BTOP to substantially increase the number of schools connected to high-speed broadband and, in turn, to substantially improve teacher training and digital learning in institutions across the country.

The ConnectED Initiative

That is why on June 6, 2013, President Obama unveiled the ConnectED initiative, a breakthrough initiative to jumpstart learning technology across our nation's K-12 schools. ConnectED will foster a robust ecosystem for digital learning, supported by robust broadband connectivity and wireless networks connecting 99% of America's K-12 students.

The ConnectED initiative will, within five years, connect 99 percent of America's students, through next-generation broadband (at speeds no less than 100Mbps and with a target of 1Gbps) to, and high-speed wireless within, their schools and libraries. The President is calling on the Federal Communications Commission (FCC) to modernize and leverage the existing E-Rate program, and leverage the expertise of the National Telecommunications and Information Administration (NTIA) to deliver this connectivity to states, districts, and schools.

Rural communities will experience some of the greatest benefits of new education technologies, as ConnectED will help provide new learning opportunities to level the playing field for rural students. The Universal Service Fund has been transformative in the past twenty years providing rural communities with telephone services, and now broadband. ConnectED builds on BTOP's successes, with greater returns for communities finding it difficult to attract broadband investment.

Innovation in Use of Wireless Spectrum

With demand for spectrum continuing to grow among both commercial and government stakeholders, President Obama remains committed to developing innovative approaches to freeing up more spectrum for wireless broadband. As recognized by the President's Council of Advisers on Science and Technology (PCAST) in its July 2012 report, *Realizing the Full Potential of Government-Held Spectrum to Spur Economic Growth*, commercial and government stakeholders must pursue and invest in emerging technologies and practices that will advance spectrum sharing and other efficiency-enhancing approaches to spectrum policy. [53]

---

[53] PCAST, "*Realizing the Full Potential of Government-Held Spectrum to Spur Economic Growth*," July 2012. Available at:
http://www.whitehouse.gov/sites/default/files/microsites/ostp/ pcast_spectrum_report_final_july_20_2012.pdf.

In some cases, Federal systems can be cleared out of a high-value spectrum band and relocated to alternative bands, allowing exclusive commercial access to the valuable band. This strategy is optimal from the perspective of the commercial service and should be pursued where feasible. But in view of the finite nature of spectrum, it is increasingly clear that the nation must augment clearing opportunities with research, development, and deployment of means to promote more spectrum sharing – part of an "all-of-the-above" approach.

Spectrum sharing can take several forms, but all involve two or more users having the right to use the same spectrum band according to rules designed to avoid interference between users. Sharing by Federal agencies maximizes spectrum efficiency and allows faster commercial access while avoiding relocation costs. Some types of sharing are already in common use, while other potentially more promising approaches are being developed and tested. They include:

- **Temporal sharing,** when one user is authorized to use a band of spectrum in some fixed geographic area at certain times and another user has access to the same band at other times.

- **Geographic sharing,** where the government designates particular protection zones restricting commercial access to a particular spectrum band in certain areas, e.g. in the proximity of a military base or a federal satellite receiver.

- **Geo-location/database-enabled sharing,** by which wireless broadband devices use available "white spaces," or gaps, in bands and locations that are allocated to other uses, but only as directed by specific location-aware technologies and databases.

- **Dynamic sensing,** which is emerging as a commercially viable approach as it receives growing attention and investment, and allows networks and devices to react in real time, detecting and moving among a wide range of available spectrum bands in accordance with agreed-upon protocols and priorities.

The continued development and deployment of spectrum sharing, in any of its forms, requires enhanced collaboration between commercial and government users, in the manner that NTIA has been overseeing for the last few years. Sharing of data regarding sensitive government systems presents risks for federal agencies, and they are to be applauded for their efforts to avoid undue risks while still moving in the direction of greater transparency as well as joint spectrum monitoring and testing with the commercial sector.

To accelerate these efforts, the Administration has released a new Presidential Memorandum, *Expanding America's Leadership in Wireless Innovation,* which promotes efficiency, transparency, and collaboration. Building on the recommendations made last year by the PCAST, the memorandum requires Federal agencies to justify system acquisitions and requests for new spectrum assignments in terms of spectrum efficiency and to improve the accuracy of their reporting on spectrum usage. It also directs agencies to increase their collaboration and data-sharing with the private sector and opens up Federal facilities to greater public-private research and development. A newly-formed White House Spectrum Policy Team will oversee implementation of the memorandum and make further recommendations as to spectrum efficiency. In addition, the Administration continues to allocate Federal funding to research and development in spectrum sharing and other advanced communications technologies. Efforts such as these will unleash even greater innovation by our nation's inventors and entrepreneurs as America continues to lead the way in wireless technologies.